Raptures and Resurrections

UNRAVELING THE LABYRINTH OF SUPER-NATURAL EVENTS

An Expose on the Reality of Life After Death

"One life to live, t'will soon
be past . . .
only what's done concerning
Christ will last."

Robert E. Daley

The Larry Czerwonka Company, LLC
Hilo, Hawai'i

Copyright © 2014 by Robert E. Daley

All rights reserved. No part of this book may be reproduced or transmitted in any form or by any means without written permission from the author.

First Edition — July 2014

Published by: The Larry Czerwonka Company
http://thelarryczerwonkacompany.com

Printed in the United States of America

ISBN: 0692247831
ISBN-13: 978-0692247839

All scriptures used in this work are taken from the
King James Version of the Scriptures.

Books by Robert E. Daley

A Case for "Threes"
A Simple Plan . . . of Immense Complexity
Armour, Weapons, And Warfare
from Everlasting to Everlasting
Killer Sex
Life or Death, Heaven or Hell, You Choose!
Raptures and Resurrections
Short Tales
So . . . What Happens to the Package?
Study and Interpretation of The Scriptures Made Simple
Surviving Destruction as A Human Being
The Gospel of John
The Gospel of John (Red Edition)
The League of The Immortals
The New Testament - Pauline Revelation
The New Testament - Pauline Revelation Companion
"The World That Then Was . . ." & The Genesis That Now Is . . .
What Color Are You?
What Makes A Christian Flaky?
What Really Happened to Judas Iscariot?
Who YOU Are in Christ . . . RIGHT NOW!

The Enhancement Series

#1 Book of Ecclesiastes
#2 Book of Daniel
#3 Book of Romans
#4 Book of Galatians
#5 Book of Hebrews

The Deeper Things of God Series

#1 The Personage of God
#2 The Personage of Man
#3 The Personage of Christ

Contents

INTRODUCTION 1

Chapter One **The Need for Resurrection** 3

Chapter Two **What is the Difference Between a Rapture and a Resurrection?** 8

Chapter Three **Two Resurrection Possibilities** 12

Chapter Four **The First and Second Raptures** 18

Chapter Five **Step One and Step Two of** *The First Resurrection* 23

Chapter Six **The Third and Fourth Raptures** 30

Chapter Seven **Step Three of** *The First Resurrection* **and Fifth Rapture** 34

Chapter Eight **The Sixth Rapture** 40

Chapter Nine **Step Four of** *The First Resurrection* **and The Seventh Rapture** 43

Chapter Ten **Fifth and Last Step of** *The First Resurrection* **and The Eighth and Last Rapture** 47

Chapter Eleven **The** *Resurrection Unto Damnation* 51

Raptures and Resurrections

INTRODUCTION

How old is old? To a *young child*, old might be thirty years of age. To a *middle-aged* individual, old might be seventy-five years of age. To a *senior-citizen*, old might even stretch to one-hundred years of age . . . or more.

In either case, the allocated number of years that a man or a woman currently spends upon this planet is comparatively very, very short. Click your heels together three times and blink your eyes, and it will all be over. And then what? Where do we go from here?

Where is John Wayne today? Where is Karl Marx today? Where is Liberace today? Where is Adolf Hitler today? Where is George Washington today? Where is Jesus Christ today? Where is great-great-grandpa today? Where are you going to be when your allotted time concludes, and the focal-plane shutter of your eyes dials down?

The Bible tells us that there is an everlasting eternity of *time* stretched out in front of us. Giving some serious thought about that, and considering what is going to happen to us when we far-too-quickly arrive there, would possibly be a good idea.

Walk with us, if you will, for a short stroll within the Scriptural accounts, through what has been a labyrinth to many. And let us glean what the God of all of creation has to say about events that lie ahead? You may be glad that you did.

CHAPTER ONE
The Need for Resurrection

"For since by man came death, by man came also the resurrection of the dead." (I Corinthians 15:21)

"Wherefore, as by one man sin entered into the world, and death by sin; and so death passed upon all men, for that all have sinned." (Romans 5:12)

These revelation statements, made by the Apostle Paul, will be the very foundation statements of our study.

Paul reveals to the believers at Rome that the stark reality of the condition of **Death**, both spiritual and physical, operates within this world of ours because of only *one man*. And if we studied it out, we would find that one man to be Adam. (Romans 5:12) And to the believers at the city of Corinth he also reveals, that because a man is responsible for the condition of **Death** affecting the entire human race, that a resurrection from that condition of **Death** must come about by another man as well. (I Corinthians 15:21)

As noted above, there is a real condition of **Spiritual Death**, as well as the well known condition of **Physical Death**. So, let us address that **Spiritual Death** issue first.

Spiritual Death

God informed Adam that there would be the consequence of **Death** for disobedience, and failure to hearken to His command. *(Genesis 2:17)* When Adam willfully chose to disobey God, he tasted of that condition of **Spiritual Death** immediately, and then, 930 years later he tasted of the reality of **Physical Death**. *(Genesis 5:5)*

That condition of **Spiritual Death** was quite real, and when it occurred, it severed the invisible, spiritual, communication umbilical, that extended from God to His finest creation endeavor, which would allow Him to communicate with His Man, Spirit to spirit.

Ergo . . . . all of Mankind has been in a **Spiritually Dead** condition, and separated from God, since the days of Adam and Eve, and there was nothing that Adam, or any man, could effectively do to change that reality. Which is why during the days of his ministry here on this Earth, Jesus of Nazareth informed a religious ruling Pharisee, named Nicodemus, that:

". . . Verily, verily, I say unto thee, Except a man be born again, (within his personal spirit) he cannot see (or understand) the kingdom of God." (John 3:3)

and

". . . Verily, verily, I say unto thee, Except a man be born of water (from a physical birth) and (born-again) of the (Holy) Spirit (within his own personal spirit), he cannot enter into the kingdom of God." (John 3:5)

CHAPTER ONE

[Enhancement added by the author to conform with truth and Scriptural continuity]

The condition of **Spiritual Death** is a serious issue which is usually not given a whole lot of thought by the average individual, because a person cannot *feel* their spirit.

In reality, as Human Beings, we are designed as a triune creature, initially physically birthed into a **Spiritually Dead** condition.

The soul portion of our being is very much alive, and will be in the *driver's seat* much sooner than we may realize, or even care to deal with.

And the physical body portion is alive, and can hardly wait to dive into all of the physical pleasures and satisfactions that it can handle during the growth process.

But the spirit portion of every individual is, technically-speaking, dead because of Sins' effect on Man, and it is like carrying around an empty sack with us wherever we go. We *sense* that there really is something there, and even feel from the time that we are extremely young that everything may not be just quite right. But we simply cannot put our finger on what it might be.

This is why it is extremely vital for the spirit of every single individual on this planet to be *birthed* again into a condition of **Spiritual Life**, from as young an age as may be possible.

And we are not talking about religion here. World-wide, there are countless religions that Mankind has created and established. However, within the totality of them all, there is not even one religious individual who does not qualify for the privileges extended, concerning actually being a Human Being: with a spirit, a soul, and a body. And that portion of the individual that is known of as his *spirit* is desperately in need of being delivered from the condition of **Spiritual Death,** by being *birthed* into a condition of **Spiritual Life,** through the placing of one's trust in the finished work of the Lord Jesus Christ of Nazareth.

May the Lord, help us to recognize the importance of that truth.

Physical Death

May this troubling issue of the condition of **Physical Death** truly fall into the category of a *no-brainer?* How many individuals from the Civil War years have you personally met? How many persons from the time of Prohibition do you know? How many Human Beings from the Dark Ages are living in New York and eating at your favorite restaurant? *(Don't answer that.)*

Everybody seems to die, do they not? Sooner or later . . . everybody seems to die. Whether that person wants to die or not . . . at some point in time, everybody dies.

The very legitimate question is . . . **WHY?**

Go and ask the scientists. They think that they surely have all, or at least most, of the answers. They cannot tell you.

Go and ask the doctors. They think that they have the messianic power of life and death, and know everything that has to do with medicine and of all things physical. They cannot tell you.

Go and ask the educators of this world. They profess themselves to be wise, and are supposed to be intelligent. They cannot tell you either. *(Romans 1:20-23)*

But the God of grace knows. The condition of **Physical Death** follows the condition of **Spiritual Death** because of the operational laws of the universe. Whether that condition of **Physical Death** occurs right away, or 969 years later, as is the case of a man named Methuselah, *(Genesis 5:27)* nevertheless, the condition of **Physical Death** will always follow the condition of **Spiritual Death** . . . always.

Should one be able to repair the inescapable problem of **Spiritual Death**, then the additional problem of needed repair for the condition of **Physical Death** will certainly follow.

The condition of **Death** is not of God. The condition of **Death** has never been of God. The foul reality of **Death** is not an operational *friend* of God. In fact, **"the last enemy that shall be destroyed, is death."** *(I Corinthians 15:26)*

So, it would be to our advantage to investigate how we might be able to side-step this heinous condition of **Death**, both spiritual and physical, and discover the simple steps that we are able to take, to assure us of the blessing of everlasting *Life*.

CHAPTER TWO
What is the Difference Between a Rapture and a Resurrection?

Webster's Ninth New Collegiate Dictionary defines **Rapture** as: *1. a state or experience of being carried away by overwhelming emotion. 2. a mystical experience in which the spirit is exalted to a knowledge of divine things. 3. an expression or manifestation of ecstasy or passion.*

None of these explanations from Mr. Webster precisely pinpoint the experience that we are Scripturally talking about. From a Scriptural layman's perspective: a *rapture* would be a carrying or catching away, in a rapid manner, of a given person from off of the surface of this planet Earth, to another locale somewhere within this created universe.

The Logos, Blueprint, Scriptural, historical-records that we have received from God indicates that at various times, in days gone by, certain individuals have experienced a swift removal from the surface of this planet, unto an unknown location. Those same records also indicate, that at some point in time, in the future, we will see the return of those same individuals to this planet once again. Where they may have gone, and what they may have been doing during their time of absence is, in most cases, unknown. There are many postulations by men of course, but no sound Scriptural testimony is actually available concerning those postulations.

CHAPTER TWO

Conjecture would declare that all of them went to *heaven*. But that conjecture is an impossibility, Scripturally speaking, because *heaven* was effectively *closed for repairs* concerning Mankind, from the days of Adam and Eve, until the resurrection of the Lord Jesus Christ. The Law of Sin had illustratively *welded* the doors shut for men because of Adam's willful disobedience, until Jesus Christ of Nazareth arose from the dead and kicked them open again.

Webster's Ninth New Collegiate Dictionary defines **Resurrection** as: *1. act of rising from the dead. 2. to rise from the dead. 3. to rise again. 4. the rising of Christ from the dead. 5. the rising again to life of all the human dead before the final judgment. 6. the state of one risen from the dead.*

Mr. Webster got it right on this one. Resurrection is undeniably connected to the state, or the condition of **Death**. And we are not talking about the condition of **Spiritual Death** here, but rather the ultimate consequence of that spiritual condition, which is the undeniable condition of **Physical Death**.

Within this world's multiple options of belief systems, there is a blatant fallacy that is put forth under the heading of *reincarnation*. The idea being that an individual on this planet, during their tenure here, failed to accomplish a requirement of self-advancement. Therefore, when the condition of **Physical Death** finally removes them from the scene, they will experience the process of *reincarnation*, and shall return to this Earth, and receive a second, or a third, or a fourth chance to *get it right*. This belief goes completely against Scriptural declaration, and sadly leads all too many spiritually ignorant persons into everlasting destruction.

There has only been one genuine *incarnation* to begin with, within the whole of time. And that was when the Second Person of the Godhead put on an Earth-suit, and became the man named Jesus Christ of Nazareth. And when, within the course of time, he physically died, he was not *reincarnated*, but rather was physically resurrected from the dead.

Resurrection is the divine process by which a physical human body is *restored* to its' previous physical condition, or *glorified* into an improved condition, for the purpose of everlasting activities.

Resurrection for individuals that have availed themselves of God's *Willy-Wonka-Golden-Ticket* offer of *Life in Christ Jesus* shall be substantially different from individuals who have refused that glorious offer. However, we shall touch upon that issue within the course of our study.

As a post-script, there is also a Scriptural notation of the action of *translation*.

Rapture - is the process of being swiftly removed from this planet Earth, and relocated to an unknown locale somewhere else within this universe.

Reincarnation - is a misnomer and an outright lie. The very postulation of reincarnation has absolutely no validity, concerning this life or of the life that is to come in the world hereafter.

CHAPTER TWO

Resurrection - is the process of physically dying, and then, at the appropriate time, being raised up from that **Physical Death** condition unto life once again.

Translation - is the process by which an individual is relocated from a point A location on this Earth, to a point B location, somewhere else on this same planet.

It is important that we have clarity concerning these very real occurrences, of which we are going to be participants. "Ignorance is **not** bliss," and we do not want to be caught unaware, when our time on this planet has run its course. The everlasting that lies out ahead, is going to be far too long to play around with.

May we soberly consider what is being presented within these pages.

CHAPTER THREE
Two Resurrection Possibilities

"Marvel not at this: for the hour is coming in the which all that are in the graves shall hear his voice,
    And shall come forth; they that have done good, unto the resurrection of life; and they that have done evil, unto the resurrection of damnation." (John 5:28-29)

From the lips of a man who never lies, Jesus of Nazareth says, there will be two distinct resurrections: One resurrection will be unto *Life*, and one resurrection will be unto *Damnation*.

And when he declares that the criteria for these resurrections is a matter of *good* or *evil*, please understand that his criteria reference is not going to be based upon what you or I may think is *good* or *evil*. "But, I'm a good person," does not even come into the picture. The foundation criteria is ultimately going to be based upon being *born-again* within one's own personal spirit, or not.

So, what is the difference between these two resurrections, and what do we have to do to qualify for the one resurrection that leads us unto *Life*?

"There was a certain rich man, which was clothed in purple and fine linen, and fared sumptuously every day.
    And there was a certain beggar named Lazarus, which was laid at his gate, full of sores,

CHAPTER THREE

And desiring to be fed with the crumbs which fell from the rich man's table: moreover the dogs came and licked his sores.

And it came to pass, that the beggar died, and was carried by the angels into Abraham's bosom: the rich man also died, and was buried;

And in hell he lift up his eyes, being in torments, and seeth Abraham afar off, and Lazarus in his bosom.

And he cried and said, Father Abraham, have mercy on me, and send Lazarus, that he may dip the tip of his finger in water, and cool my tongue; for I am tormented in this flame.

But Abraham said, Son, remember that thou in thy lifetime receivedst thy good things, and likewise Lazarus evil things: but now he is comforted, and thou art tormented.

And beside all this, between us and you there is a great gulf fixed: so that they which would pass from hence to you cannot; neither can they pass to us, that would come from thence.

Then he said, I pray thee therefore, father, that thou wouldst send him to my father's house:

For I have five brethren; that he may testify unto them, lest they also come into this place of torment.

Abraham saith unto him, They have Moses and the prophets; let them hear them.

And he said, Nay, father Abraham: but if one went unto them from the dead, they will repent.

And he said unto him, If they hear not Moses and the prophets, neither will they be persuaded, though one rose from the dead." (Luke 16:19-31)

This incident that is being relayed to us is not a parable. In reality, this is a true story that Jesus Christ of Nazareth is telling us, concerning two Jewish individuals who are in a Blood Covenant relationship with the Living God, and at differing points in time, both of them physically die. This is a story that we should not ignore nor treat lightly. We should become very familiar with the details, and insight, that God is graciously giving unto us concerning the *Nether World*, or *World of Departed Spirits*, or *Hell* as it is commonly referred to today. This locale of *Hell* is the area that was originally **"prepared for the devil and his angels,"** (Matthew 25:41) but it will work just as well for the disobedient and rebellious individuals of Mankind.

Both of these men went to *Hell*, of a necessity, because heaven had been *closed for repairs* ever since Adam and Eve had chosen to disobey God and had willfully sinned. After their physical demise, God is going to have to have some place to keep these men in their deceased condition. So you have one of the compartments, out of five, in the *Nether World* complex that is within the bowels of this planet, that holds the people that, through the ages, have believed on God and did *good* while they were on the Earth; and a second of those five compartments within the same abode that holds the people that, through the same ages, did not believe God and did not do *good* while they were on this earth, but rather were *evil*.

CHAPTER THREE

It is very important that we keep in mind that this story, and what happened to these men, happened before the death and resurrection of the Lord Jesus Christ; because his resurrection from the conditions of being spiritually and physically dead is what changed everything.

Now, please understand that confusion may potentially arise if we do not have clarity concerning certain spiritual events and truths, that are in harmony with Scriptural declaration.

Prior to the resurrection of Jesus Christ of Nazareth, all men, living anywhere on this planet, were in a **Spiritually Dead** condition. One nation, and one nation only, was in a Blood Covenant relationship with the Living God. All of the men, from every other nation on Earth, were not in any covenant condition. Long ago God attempted to commission the whole nation of Israel to become priests, and mediate between Himself and every other nation on the planet so that all the men from those nations might have an opportunity to know the truth—but Israel refused. *(Exodus 19:4-6)* So, what is God going to do from there, since they have a free-will? And when asked to help, they said *No!* to His request.

Ergo, within the nation of Israel at that time, all that any man could do, was to live and to do the very best that they knew how to do. They could do nothing more because of their involuntary servitude to sin. Thus, when a man had physically died, if he had done *good* he went into the *comfort* compartment within the *Nether World* complex . . . and if he had done *evil* he went into the *torment* compartment.

When the time came, Jesus himself went into the *torment* compartment, to pay the Sin-Indebtedness that the whole world owes. However, when that price was fully paid, Jesus was raised up from the dead, and broke the spiritual chains of Sin that kept men in bondage and in the condition of **Spiritual Death.** *(Hebrews 2:14-15)* He then went on into the *comfort* compartment, known as *Paradise* or *Abraham's Bosom*, and rescued the beggar that we read about in our true story. When Jesus himself was physically resurrected from the dead, the beggar was also physically resurrected shortly thereafter according to God's testimony. *(Matthew 27:52-53)*

Today, there is a new Blood Covenant that men can belong to—and the personal, spiritual *New-Birth* of an individual, is the key-of-entrance to that Covenant. And it is also the criteria for *Resurrection unto Life, (John 5:29)* which is no longer simply based upon being, or doing *good*, or upon being, or doing *evil*. Today, it is mandatory that one must be *born-again* within one's own personal spirit. And if one is a participant of the *New-Birth*, then that one becomes a candidate for the *First Resurrection*. And if one is not a participant of the *New-Birth*—then no matter how *religious* one may be—one automatically becomes a candidate for the *Resurrection unto Damnation*.

Because of the numerous details that are involved within the whole of the Plan of Redemption, the fulfillment of the first, *Resurrection unto Life* reality, shall consist of five segments or *events*.

The second, *Resurrection unto Damnation* reality, shall consist of only one final event, at the appointed time.

CHAPTER THREE

Throughout the remainder of our study, we shall purpose to note and observe the various *Raptures* and *Resurrections* that shall occur prior to the launching-out of humanity into the everlasting ahead.

CHAPTER FOUR
The First and Second Raptures

"And all the days of Enoch were three hundred sixty and five years:
And Enoch walked with God: and he was not; for God took him." (Genesis 5:23-24)

Enoch

Approximately five thousand years ago, a man named Enoch chose to believe what he had been told about the God of all creation. He was a man who was in the condition of being **Spiritually Dead** in his sins, but he had faith to believe God.

Within the Logos, Blueprint, Scriptural, Historical-records it is decreed that God will graciously provide Two Witnesses, (Revelation 11:3) to testify of His truth, amid the courts of the Antichrist, as a last-chance opportunity of salvation, within the prophesied Tribulation Period. God must get these Two Witnesses from somewhere . . . so the first one that is chosen by God is a *Gentile* man named Enoch. He comes from before the Flood of Noah, and is familiar with the wickedness of men's hearts desiring to do evil continually. (Genesis 6:5) He will be a perfect witness for the wickedness that shall abound during the days of Antichrist.

From the nominal amount of Scriptural information that we have on Enoch, it can be concluded that God is the One who actually did the *rapturing*, but Enoch is the one who released the faith for it to legally take place.

Normally, it is Scripturally spoken of, that Enoch was *translated*. However, from our definitions for the purpose of this study, we have seen that a translation is from one point of location on this planet, to another point of location; and Enoch was *raptured* from one point of location on this planet, to an unknown point of location somewhere within the universe.

Today, Enoch is still Physically Alive . . . somewhere, and has been for the last five-thousand years. This author, for lack of space to expound fully, believes that Enoch has been brought into a close-proximity to God, but is unable to live and abide with God, because, at the time of his *rapturing*, he was yet **Spiritually Dead** in his sins, and heaven was *closed for repairs* to the spiritually dead, as a result of the Law of Sin actively operating within the Earth. However, he must return at some point in time, to fulfill the Scripture, and to become spiritually *born-again*, and to physically die.

Elijah

"And Elijah took his mantle, and wrapped it together, and smote the waters, and they were divided hither and thither, so that they two went over on dry ground.

And it came to pass, when they were gone over, that Elijah said unto Elisha, Ask what I shall do for thee, be-

fore I be taken away from thee. And Elisha said, I pray thee, let a double portion of thy spirit be upon me.

And he said, Thou hast asked a hard thing: nevertheless, if thou see me when I am taken from thee, it shall be so unto thee; but if not, it shall not be so.

And it came to pass, as they still went on, and talked, that, behold, there appeared a chariot of fire, and horses of fire, and parted them both asunder; and Elijah went up by a whirlwind into heaven.

And Elisha saw it, and he cried, My father, my father, the chariot of Israel, and the horsemen thereof. And he saw him no more. And he took hold of his own clothes, and rent them in two pieces." (II Kings 2:8-12)

The second Scriptural account of a *rapture* occurred approximately some fifteen hundred years after Enoch's removal from the Earth. A prophet from the Nation of Israel, a *Jewish* man named Elijah, was informed of his departure, and removed from the face of the planet by a fiery chariot.

Many Bible scholars, when teaching on *end-time* events and the Book of Revelation, declare that Elijah and Moses are actually the Two Witnesses that were mentioned earlier within this work. Or, Elijah and John the Baptist are put forward as the candidates.

To be sure, Elijah is one of the elect two, because the prophet Malachi reveals that truth within his writings. But Moses, or John the Baptist, or some other outstanding individual is normally named as the second candidate because of

CHAPTER FOUR

the miracles that they did, or the signs and wonders that followed them.

The Scriptures reveal clearly that the Living God that we serve is a God of Covenant, and Covenant is paramount. Dealings that we read about within the Old Testament, for the most part, are dealings that occurred between God and His Blood Covenant Chosen people of the Nation of Israel.

Within the New Testament, the dealings that we read about in the epistles, that have been preserved for us, are dealings between God and His Blood Covenant *children-of-adoption*, through Jesus Christ of Nazareth. These revealed truths and dealings are not simply actions between God and the entire world. There is no Blood Covenant at all, actively in operation between God and the people of this world that we live in. But the finality issue of physical resurrection-from-the-dead, which is our chosen subject, definately affects every single Human Being on the face of the planet who has physically died.

This author is persuaded that indeed Elijah is the individual that God has chosen to be the representative, within these *last-days-&-end-times* happenings, and for the purpose of resurrection legalities, for every single subject who is in a Covenantal relationship with God, through blood.

God was not ever in any type of Blood Covenant relationship with the Gentile, Enoch. So, for the express purpose of final resurrection legalities, God has chosen him to be the representative of every single subject who is not bound by blood in a Covenantal relationship with Himself.

The conclusion of the matter is just this . . . using the process of a *rapture*, God has selected two individuals from days gone by, that will play a key part in the necessary probational events of the *last days*; and all of the very real resurrection legalities that need be in place, to complete creative Divine design . . . whether the individual *free-will* choice of Man is ultimately to obey or to disobey the eternal premise.

CHAPTER FIVE
Step One and Step Two of The First Resurrection

From the days of Adam and Eve, to the days of Jesus Christ of Nazareth, no further *raptures* have taken place other than the two occurrences of Enoch and Elijah. And within that same four-thousand year span of time, no resurrections have occurred, at all. The New Testament Scriptures declare quite plainly, the spiritual reality that:

> **"And as it is appointed unto men once to die, but after this the judgment:"** *(Hebrews 9:27)*

And even though this Scriptural statement of truth itself, is declared after the universe-altering event of the resurrection of Jesus Christ of Nazareth from the dead . . . still, the Scriptures cannot be broken. Legally and technically speaking, any individual within the Logos, Blueprint, Old Testament, Historical-record accounts who *seemingly* physically died and then was brought back to life again, whatever the mitigating circumstances may have been, was not really resurrected again unto life, but rather was actually *healed*. And, even if we do not personally understand why, or know how that it was done, the truth of it is not altered whatsoever.

"I will declare the decree: the Lord hath said unto me, Thou art my Son, this day have I begotten thee." (Psalm 2:7)

"God hath fulfilled the same unto us their children, in that he hath raised up Jesus again; as it is also written in the second psalm, Thou art my Son, this day have I begotten thee." (Acts 13:33)

"In whom we have redemption through his blood, even the forgiveness of sins:
Who is the image of the invisible God, the firstborn of every (New) creature:" (Colossians 1:14-15)

[Enhancement added by the author to conform with truth and Scriptural continuity]

"And he is the head of the body, the church: who is the beginning, the firstborn from the (spiritual) dead; that in all things he might have the preeminence." (Colossians 1:18)

[Enhancement added by the author to conform with truth and Scriptural continuity]

"And from Jesus Christ, who is the faithful witness, and the first-begotten of the (spiritual) dead, and the prince of the kings of the earth. Unto him that loved us, and washed us from our sins in his own blood." (Revelation 1:5)

CHAPTER FIVE

[Enhancement added by the author to conform with truth and Scriptural continuity]

"And unto the angel of the church of the Laodiceans write; These things saith the Amen, the faithful and true witness, the beginning of the *(New)* creation of God." *(Revelation 3:14)*

[Enhancement added by the author to conform with truth and Scriptural continuity]

These six Scriptural accounts are only a few that testify as to what was prophesied in the Old Testament, and fulfilled with the universe-altering event that we know of as the resurrection of the Lord Jesus Christ, from both the spiritual and physical conditions of **Death**. *(Hebrews 2:9)*

The understanding of the situation should not take rocket-science for us to grasp, if we are willing to hear and receive the truth:

- God purposes to create an **in** Our image and **after** Our likeness creature *(Genesis 1:26)* . . . that is an **express image** of His own Person *(Hebrews 1:3)* . . . and unprecedented in original design. That individual is going to be a spirit being, just like God. *(John 4:24)*
- The active operation of the Law of Sin *(which is already in existence at the time of Adam and Eve)* is brought back into the Earth by the first Man, Adam, and allowed to function again for a second time. *(Romans 5:12)*
- Adam and Eve fall prey to seduction and disobedience, and the condition of **Spiritual Death** is the im-

mediate result; *(Genesis 2:17)* but that **Spiritual Death** condition causes no disruption within the compositional make-up components of Man, at that time. *(I Thessalonians 5:23)*

- Within the passage of time, the condition of **Physical Death** follows the condition of **Spiritual Death**, and when that happens a triunity disruption does indeed occur between the spirit, and the soul, and the body compositional components, that constitute the make-up of a Human-Being.
- The solution for the condition of **Spiritual Death** is a ***Spiritual Rebirth***. That will be accomplished through the finished work of the cross by the Lord Jesus Christ of Nazareth; and is also why a man *must* be born-again in order to establish an individual identification with Christ. *(John 3:3 & 5)*
- The solution for the condition of **Physical Death** is a bodily ***Resurrection*** of the affected individual. That will also be accomplished through the finished work of the cross of the Lord Jesus. *(I Corinthians 15:21-22)*

At the appropriate prophesied time, the work of the cross of Christ, accomplishes the first necessity of ***Spiritual Rebirth*** that has ever occurred. *(Colossians 1:18)* Within the bowels of the complex of the *Nether World*, Jewish Jesus Christ of Nazareth was *birthed* into the **New Creation** Jesus, whom after the flesh, *"know we him no more."* *(II Corinthians 5:16)*

Very shortly after this universe-altering event is completed, the physical body of Jesus experiences the first physical resurrection on record, in being raised up unto ***Physical Life***.

(Revelation 3:14) Step One of the *bodily-resurrection-reality-necessity* process is now complete. *(I Corinthians 15:23)*

"And, behold, the veil of the temple was rent in twain from the top to the bottom; and the earth did quake, and the rocks rent;

And the graves were opened; and many bodies of the saints which slept arose,

And came out of the graves after his resurrection, and went into the holy city, and appeared unto many."
(Matthew 27:51-53)

Matthew's testimony of truth establishes the foundational basis for Step Two of the designed *bodily-resurrection* process. Jesus of Nazareth indeed *cut-the-trail* as far as providing for a new **Spiritual Rebirth**, and having the physical body of a man to be resurrected unto life again as well. But there were other individuals also that were waiting in line.

Since the time of Adam and Eve, men and women who believed what God had said, as few as there may have been, and who lived the very best that they could, when they died would still not be able to go into heaven. They were carried, by the angels, as the beggar was, into *Abraham's Bosom*, which was the comfort compartment within the *Nether World* complex. *(Luke 16:22)* There they waited together, century after century, until the *"fulness of the time"* should come. *(Galatians 4:4)*

When Jesus completed the necessary, mandatory payment of an extensive debt that all men owed, *(Romans 6:23)* new legalities were freshly established, and he made the *New Birth* process a **Spiritual Life** reality. With the individual, personal *spirit* issue being effectively dealt with, a way was now paved for a physical resurrection of the body to take place. For clarity's sake, the order of *event* occurrence is as follows:

- While in the *citadel of the damned*, Jesus is birthed from a condition of **Spiritual Death** unto a condition of **Spiritual Life** by the power of the Holy Spirit of God. *(Acts 2:24 & Hebrews 2:9)* And with that new Spiritual Birth condition, a new Spiritual Law is established. *(Romans 8:2)*
- Jesus is then physically raised up from the dead to the condition of **Physical Life** once again, by the power of the same Holy Spirit of God. *(Acts 2:27)*
- All of the men and women within the *Paradise* or *Abraham's Bosom* compartment of the *Nether World*, who went there from the time of Adam and Eve, until the time of the resurrection of Jesus Christ, are then born-again unto new **Spirit Life**, when Jesus presents himself as the promised Messiah, preaches to them, and grants unto them the power to become the *sons of God*. *(John 1:12)*
- Because there is now a new Spiritual Law in place . . . the Law of *Life in Christ Jesus* *(Romans 8:2)* . . . heaven has been *re-opened* for business once again. The complex locale of *Hell* cannot legally hold on to its centuries old captives any more. So Jesus is able to lead **"captivity captive"** *(Ephesians 4:8)* when he leaves the *Nether World* complex to return to the surface of this planet and continue to fulfill prophetical declaration.
- According to the Scripture quoted above, many of these now free resurrected individuals went into the

CHAPTER FIVE

holy city of Jerusalem, after the resurrection of Jesus, and appeared to family and friends. *(Matthew 27:51-53)* Step One and Step Two of the *First Resurrection* event are now complete.

CHAPTER SIX
The Third and Fourth Raptures

"And when he had spoken these things, while they beheld, he was taken up; and a cloud received him out of their sight." (Acts 1:9)

The man Jesus Christ of Nazareth is the human instrument that God utilized to accomplish needed **Spiritual Rebirth** and the foundational, precedent-setting **Physical Resurrection**, for all of the members of Mankind that experience **Physical Death**, during the probational period. He is also the focused object of the third *rapture*.

The two Human men, Enoch and Elijah, were removed from this Earth, for the purpose of future prophetical fulfillment, and have been *preserved* by God, somewhere within the confines of this universe. Since they cannot yet legally live with God in heaven because of their **Spiritual Deadness** conditon, and since there is no Scriptural indication of any of God's *air-to-breathe*, *food-to-eat*, *clothes-to-wear*, and the *other-necessities* provision, spoken of anywhere . . . may this author suggest a *science-fiction* proposal of a *close-to-God-time-suspended-difference-between-an-inhale-and-an-exhale* consideration?

However, whatever the reality of resolve might be for Enoch and Elijah, the resurrected Jesus Christ of Nazareth is the third candidate for the actions involving *raptures*.

CHAPTER SIX

Upon his First Coming to this Earth, Jesus of Nazareth was rejected by the very nation that he came to save. Scripture will bear out that prior to his being soundly refused as the prophesied Messiah by the leadership of Israel, Jesus only came to redeem the people of the Nation of Israel, in fulfillment of Abrahamic Covenant given promises, and the rescuing of the heirs of covenant declarations.

"But he answered and said, I am not sent but unto the lost sheep of the house of Israel." (Matthew 15:24)

"For the Son of man is come to save that which was lost." (Matthew 18:11)

"These twelve Jesus sent forth, and commanded them, saying, Go not into the way of the Gentiles, and into any city of the Samaritans enter ye not:
But go rather to the lost sheep of the house of Israel."
(Matthew 10:5-6)

"He came unto his own, and his own received him not." (John 1:11)

"Now I say that Jesus Christ was a minister of the circumcision for the truth of God, to confirm the promises made unto the fathers:" (Romans 15:8)

These six declarations alone, from three different authors, should settle the issue concerning the validity of the doctrine of original salvation for the Nation of Israel only.

And because the Nation of Israel did not receive him at the first, there is still a prophetical future work to be fulfilled with the people of Israel. When we read within the Book of Revelation, concerning the Nation of Israel, and the Millennial Reign of Christ, we are witnessing the resumption of what Jesus came to do in the first place, concerning the Chosen People of God.

When Jesus Christ of Nazareth was raised from the condition of being dead, both **Spiritually** and **Physically**, a whole new program was started. It is known as the **New Creation Project**. And, concerning the **C**hief **E**xecutive **O**fficer of this program, we are not just dealing with a Human Being *remodel* in the resurrected Jesus . . . we are dealing with something that is brand new . . . a **New Creation**. Jesus is no longer a natural-Jewish man, he is a born-again, resurrected, recreated, immortal, super-natural, **New Creation** man.

From the *time* of his Physical Resurrection until the *time* of his Second Coming, the element of *time* is Scripturally known of as the *Time of the Gentiles*. And during that *time* there is a whole new set of operating parameters that we are involved with concerning spiritual issues, that we do not have the space to get into here.

However, ultimately Jesus must still fulfill promises that were made to God's Chosen People under the Abrahamic Blood Covenant. So, he will return to this Earth in order to accomplish that legal necessity at his Second Coming. And, just like Enoch and Elijah, Jesus of Nazareth is the third person to be *raptured* from off of this planet, in preparation for future prophetical fulfillment.

CHAPTER SIX

In addition, because the resurrection of Jesus was a universe-altering, calendar-changing event, we are at a transition point. *Old* things, specifically concerning issues dealing with the Nation of Israel, are being moved to the *back burner* of the stove, from heaven's perspective; and all of the *New* things, concerning all of the issues dealing with the Blood Covenant **New Creation**, are beginning to take place.

One of those *New* things that are taking place right at the get-go is the *New-Birth* and *Physical Resurrection* of those individuals from the days of Adam and Eve, who had received and believed what God had said, and lived in hope of the promises. At this point in *time*, being liberated in body and in spirit from the Paradise compartment, they no longer have a place on this Earth, but are destined to live with God in heaven. So, during the first forty days after the precedent-setting event of Jesus' resurrection, they have been granted *leave* to return to family and friends for the purpose of encouragement of promise-fulfillment-substantiation from a loving God. *(Matthew 27:52-53)* And when Jesus is *raptured* ten days before The Feast of Pentecost, they transition to heaven as well. However, valid Scriptural notation is silent on their leaving because the focus is not on them, it is on Jesus.

CHAPTER SEVEN
Step Three of The First Resurrection and Fifth Rapture

"For the Lord himself shall descend from heaven with a shout, with the voice of the archangel, and with the trump of God: and the dead in Christ shall rise first:

Then we which are alive and remain shall be caught up together with them in the clouds, to meet the Lord in the air: and so shall we ever be with the Lord." (I Thessalonians 4:16-17)

"Behold, I show you a mystery, We shall not all sleep, but we shall all be changed.

In a moment, in the twinkling of an eye, at the last trump: for the trumpet shall sound, and the dead shall be raised incorruptible, and we shall be changed.

For this corruption must put on incorruption, and this mortal must put on immortality." (I Corinthians 15:51-53)

Of all of the *events* that we are addressing within this little work, this particular *event* is the most well-known amongst Christians today. Not that there is a real clarity within all of Christianity concerning exactly what all is going to happen, but, it is the most well-known.

The two Scriptural segments quoted above from the apostle Paul, are but the major notations of insight concerning this

CHAPTER SEVEN 35

event. Other references can be found in various locations within both the *Old* and the *New* Testaments.

From the days of Enoch and Elijah, until the days of Jesus of Nazareth, there were no further *raptures* and no resurrections at all. The removal by *rapture* purpose for them is for the necessary future prophetical fulfillment.

Jesus himself is the originator of **Spiritual Rebirth** and is the candidate for the first **Physical Resurrection**. Upon his resurrection, the spiritual bonds of Sin were broken, and the righteous constituency from the time of Adam and Eve unto Jesus, were legally able to be *re-born* within the Paradise compartment, and raised up from being Physically Dead. At the designated time, Jesus was the third to be *raptured* for the purpose of future prophetical fulfillment, and the other resurrected righteous individuals ascended into heaven with him, becoming the fourth constituency to be *raptured*, even though there is no obvious Scriptural notation.

The *event* that we are now looking at is going to be the prophetical fulfillment of a *mystery*. And every single individual on the face of this planet who is *in Christ*, beginning from the resurrection of Jesus of Nazareth unto the actual *mystery* manifestation, is going to be affected.

Even though we have Scripturally seen that there are numerous *raptures*, this particular *event* is the one that is frequently referred to as the *Rapture of the Church*.

Human men and women, who have believed and trusted in Christ Jesus, and hence have become born-again New Creations, from the time of his resurrection and ascension until now, and have ultimately grown physically old and died, or left this Earth before the Scriptural fulfillment of their *time* allocation, or have been persecuted and martyred for their faith, have done so with expectation. At their departure, their spirit-soul essence has been carried by the holy angels into the presence of the Lord. *(II Corinthians 5:8)* This is the mystical *event* that is going to remedy all that they have endured and gone through.

From the very resurrection of Jesus Christ, the dispensational *age* that we have been living in is known of as the *Age of Grace*. Within the *Age of Grace* there is no behavioral-modification Law of Moses in operation, and there is no Wrath of God being poured out.

Although much of Christianity does not seem to understand it, *Grace* and Law or *Grace* and Wrath are not compatible, and do not mix. That does not mean to say that there are not possibly going to be *bad* things that will happen unto *good people*. We are engaged in a full-fledged spiritual war, and the enemy of God and Man does know what he is doing. However, the Word of God promises that for those individuals who are *in Christ* . . . we are not appointed unto God's Wrath *(I Thessalonians 5:9)* . . . and the very righteousness of God has been revealed unto us, and extended, without the Law. *(Romans 10:4)*

And at this point, the rest of the world, which is running at break-neck speed unto *hell in a hand basket*, will be able to benefit from the umbrella Covenant protection that all spiritual children are afforded from a loving Father . . . until the occurrence of this *event*. And then, it will all dramatically change.

CHAPTER SEVEN

Jesus of Nazareth is due to return to this planet Earth . . . twice! Once to remove the true Christians from the soon coming Tribulation Period, and once to save the Nation of Israel from destruction.

His first return is in reference to his, *"that where I am, they may be also"* prayer at the Last Supper. *(John 17:24)* And sadly, there are those in Christendom today who proclaim that they are *in Christ*, and yet desire to dismiss these Scriptures concerning the *"blessed hope"* *(Titus 2:13)* as invalid, and declare that these are not really applicable to the church. These individuals are not really looking for his return, *(Hebrews 9:28)* and so they may indeed miss it.

This first return for his own is in direct connection to the living *body* known as The Church that he is the Head of, and for those individuals who are part *"of his flesh and of his bones."* *(Ephesians 5:30)* Jesus is a **New Creation** now, and all of the other born-again **New Creatures** *(II Corinthians 5:17)* are directly connected unto him by the indwelling power of the Holy Spirit of God. The entire constituency of *believers* make up the real live spiritual Body-of-Christ.

We will be working, and ministering, and ruling with Christ Jesus within the eons that are stretched out ahead. When this *event* occurs, dispensational *Grace* will come to a conclusion and be withdrawn, and dispensational *Law* will be returned to the Nation of Israel, because that Nation of Israel is going to be brought back to the *front-burner* of God's focus. He is prophetically *not done with them yet* concerning original Covenant promises. It only makes sense that we are to be removed from the *wrath to come (Matthew 3:7 & Revelation 16:1, 19)* and taken to a place where we may continue in our being conformed into his *image* process, *(Romans 8:29)* and into the advanced classes of our on-going spiritual education.

Just a short notation for now . . . the second return of Jesus is in connection with the Nation of Israel, and the fulfillment of the last 7 year wrap-up of a 490 year prophecy that finds its origin within the Book of Daniel. *(Daniel 9:24)* But we will look more extensively at that, in greater detail, in the chapters ahead.

Today, Matthew 24:36, **"But of that day and hour knoweth no man, no, not the angels of heaven, but my Father only"** is probably the number-one, misunderstood and out-of-context quoted Scripture, within all of modern-day Christianity. It is directly following the statement that heaven and earth shall pass away, and has nothing at all to do with the *Rapture of the Church*. Professed intelligent Christians, failing to rightly divide the word of truth, *(II Timothy 2:15)* have misled millions of people concerning this major Scripturally predictable *event*.

And, please understand that there is no valid basis for *date-setting* when it comes to this controversial issue. However, we cannot simply disregard God's declaration of truth, **"Surely the Lord God will do nothing, but he revealeth his secret unto his servants the prophets"** *(Amos 3:7)*. . . . or allocate that this statement simply refers only to the Nation of Israel, either. We must be ever watchful, and attentive to what the Spirit would say unto the churches. *(Revelation 3:22)*

This *event* is personally directed, and attended to, by the Lord Jesus Christ himself. He will return to this Earth as he prayed, *(John 17:24)* and bring all of the disembodied spirit-soul individuals with him, who have physically died from the time of his resurrection-ascension until that very *event*-fulfilling moment. The *dead in Christ* bodies *(I Thessalonians 4:16)* of these saints shall then experience Step Three of the **First Resurrection**, and directly following that segment, the Fifth Rapture shall occur, which should include you and this author being caught up to meet the Lord in the air. *(I Thessalonians 4:17)* Various transitions shall occur among the saints, including, but not limited to: from corruption to incorruption . . . from physical to spiritual . . . and from mortal to immortal changes. *(I Corinthians 15:53 & 15:44-46)*

In a once-again completed triune condition, all of the saints shall then return to the Father's house with Jesus, leaving this planet vacant of even one *in Christ*, born-again, recreated, super-natural, New Creation, Christian. We shall begin to become involved with the affairs that are going on in heaven, while the *wrap-up* issues concerning the Nation of Israel and the *Tribulation Period* are continuing on this Earth.

CHAPTER EIGHT
The Sixth Rapture

The whole of planet Earth is now void of any genuine Christians. There are numerous *lukewarm* (Revelation 3:15) individuals throughout the entire surface of the globe, but predominately their concentration is going to be in the decadent Western Hemisphere.

After the *Rapture of the Church* takes place, those pseudo-Christians who find themselves still here, will gravitate in one of two distinct directions. For some, a godly sorrow and a genuine repentance will occur, and they will commit themselves fully unto the Lord Jesus, this time to the expense of their own physical life. They will refuse to recant Christ when they are pressured and persecuted by the wickedness of this world, and will ultimately end up being martyred for their faith. *(Revelation 6:9)* The second constituency of *luke warmers* will become quite bitter toward the Living God when they are *left behind*. Deluded by seducing spirits into thinking that they should have been taken in the *rapture* because they were a *good Christian*, they shall lead themselves into a condition of hardness of heart; continually rejecting an extended hand of love from a God who does not desire that even one should perish. *(II Peter 3:9)*

There is no Scripturally designated time allocation between the *Rapture of the Church* and the signing of the *one week* covenant *(Daniel 9:27) event* that starts the prophetic clock ticking

CHAPTER EIGHT

again, for the Nation of Israel. However, *grace* is now gone, and the severity of the Law is installed and operating once again, but only within the Nation of Israel. The remainder of the Earth will find themselves living in a godless condition. Early signs of godly wrath begin to seep out as the weeks and months tick by.

"And there appeared a great wonder in heaven; a woman clothed with the sun, and the moon under her feet, and upon her head a crown of twelve stars:
And she being with child cried, travailing in birth, and pained to be delivered.
And there appeared another wonder in heaven; and behold a great red dragon, having seven heads and ten horns, and seven crowns upon his heads.
And his tail drew the third part of the stars of heaven, and did cast them to the earth: and the dragon stood before the woman which was ready to be delivered, for to devour her child as soon as it was born.
And she brought forth a man child, who was to rule all nations with a rod of iron: and her child was caught up unto God, and to his throne." (Revelation 12:1-5)

This segment of Scripture is parenthetical rather than chronological. However, that does not change our focus.

During the first-half of the seven-year-long *Time of Jacob's Trouble,* (Jeremiah 30:7) *Daniel's Seventieth Week,* (Daniel 9:27) *Tribulation Period,* (Matthew 24:21) that is prophetically due to unfold upon the Jewish Nation of Israel, various individuals throughout the whole world have chosen to put their trust in Christ

Jesus. Within the whole of the Gentile world, these souls end up under the altar in heaven, as they are martyred for their faith in various locations on the Earth. *(Revelation 6:9)*

Within the focused back-on-the-front-burner Nation of Israel, 12,000 young virgin men, from each of the twelve tribes, will gladly embrace the invitation to follow the Lamb of God. These are those who are referred to as the *Man Child* within the fifth verse, of the twelfth chapter, within the Book of Revelation. These men excel in righteousness and zealousness, and they reside right in the heart of Antichrist's territory. They shall ultimately incite a spiritual irritation that blooms into a full-blown eruption that Antichrist focuses his complete attention on eliminating. *(Revelation 12:4)* As he is poised to launch a focused death blow, the Sixth Rapture *event* occurs, and the entire 144,000 *Man Child* constituency is removed from Antichrist's grasp and caught up into the Father's house in heaven. *(Revelation 12:5)* Exceeding rejoicing takes place within the New Jerusalem, as a seething wrath of intensified hatred smolders in the Middle Eastern segment of planet Earth. From this point on in time, until the conclusion of the whole matter, because the last portion of the Wrath of God is due to be poured out soon, it shall only go down-hill for this planet . . . rapidly.

CHAPTER NINE
Step Four of The First Resurrection and The Seventh Rapture

"After this I beheld, and, lo, a great multitude, which no man could number, of all nations, and kindreds, and people, and tongues, stood before the throne, and before the Lamb, clothed with white robes, and palms in their hands;

And cried with a loud voice, saying, Salvation to our God which sitteth upon the throne, and unto the Lamb.

And all the angels stood round about the throne, and about the elders and the four beasts, and fell before the throne on their faces, and worshipped God.

Saying, Amen: Blessing, and glory, and wisdom, and thanksgiving, and honour, and power, and might, be unto our God for ever and ever. Amen.

And one of the elders answered, saying unto me, What are these which are arrayed in white robes? and whence came they?

And I said unto him, Sir, thou knowest. And he said to me, These are they which came out of great tribulation, and have washed their robes, and made them white in the blood of the Lamb.

Therefore are they before the throne of God, and serve him day and night in his temple: and he that sitteth on the throne shall dwell among them.

They shall hunger no more, neither thirst any more; neither shall the sun light on them, nor any heat.

For the Lamb which is in the midst of the throne shall feed them, and shall lead them unto living fountains of water: and God shall wipe away all tears from their eyes." (Revelation 7:9-17)

"And I saw as it were a sea of glass mingled with fire: and them that had gotten the victory over the beast, and over his image, and over his mark, and over the number of his name, stand on the sea of glass, having the harps of God.

And they sing the song of Moses the servant of God, and the song of the Lamb, saying Great and marvelous are thy works, Lord God Almighty; just and true are thy ways, thou King of saints.

Who shall not fear thee, O Lord, and glorify thy name? For thou only art holy: for all nations shall come and worship before thee; for thy judgments are made manifest." (Revelation 15:2-4)

At the mid-point of the *Tribulation Period* the Antichrist makes his move.

At the mid-point of the *Tribulation Period* the 144,000 young, virgin, Hebrew males are *raptured* from off of the face of this planet, into the presence of the Lamb that they have chosen to follow.

CHAPTER NINE

At the mid-point of the *Tribulation Period* the Antichrist definitively deals with the associate religious hierarchy and the leadership of the *ten-nation confederacy* that propelled him into power; and enters into the *holiest of all* portion of the temple in Israel and commits the *abomination of desolation* that has been spoken of by Daniel the prophet, (Matthew 24:15) by proclaiming that he alone, is god.

At the mid-point of the *Tribulation Period* when the Antichrist reveals his true colors, the Nation of Israel is horrified, and will attempt to flee from the impending destruction that he will immediately order. (Matthew 24:16-20)

At the mid-point of the *Tribulation Period* the Two Witnesses of Enoch and Elijah, are returned once again to the Earth to take up where the 144,000 have left off, and fulfill prophetical Scriptural declarations.

Conditions of life throughout the whole of the Earth are becoming more and more intolerable, but particularly within the kingdom of the Antichrist, which is established within a ten-nation confederacy of Arabic countries within the Middle East. Outside of Israel as well, saints are being murdered for their faith in Christ and it is becoming quite popular to cut off their heads, in order to accomplish this goal.

This killing of Christians has been going on since the beginning of the *Tribulation Period*. After the revelation of the *Son of Perdition*, and at the mid-point of the *Seventieth Week*, the slaughter intensifies.

We do not have a Scriptural time notation as to when this butchering activity ceases. But we do know that the Scriptures tell us of a time of **"great tribulation, such as**

was not since the beginning of the world to this time, no, nor ever shall be," *(Matthew 24:21)* and that is not just referring to the *natural*, or the meteorological, or to the catastrophic occurrences that we always seem to emphasize when we refer to the Book of Revelation. It is also talking about intensified Man's inhumanity to Man, which always finds its origin at the seat of Satan.

We also know that the early part of the *tribulation martyrs* *(Revelation 6:9)* were told to **"rest yet for a little season, until their fellow servants also and their brethren . . . should be killed as they were."** *(Revelation 6:11)* So we should be able to discern that when this occurs, the time for the fulfillment is near.

The *Tribulation Period* itself is Scripturally, 2,520 days long, from the signing of the *covenant* agreement unto the returning of Jesus Christ to this Earth known as the *Second Coming*. The *event* of our next chapter, potentially occurs just days before that *Second Coming* event. So it is reasonable to consider that the unceremonious, unnoticed, and *invisible* event of the simultaneous Fourth Step of the *First Resurrection* and the seventh *rapture* might take place just days before the more well-known final Two Witness' death, resurrection, and removal from this Earth.

CHAPTER TEN
Fifth and Last Step of The First Resurrection and The Eighth and Last Rapture

It is during the 1,260 days first-half part of the *Tribulation Period*, that the young virgin Jewish men shall begin to receive *New-Life* in Christ Jesus. As their numbers increase so does their zealousness. The spot-light of heaven is once again on the Nation of Israel within the Middle-East, and because God will not leave His people without a witness for righteousness, these young men have become the representation for His holiness and righteousness to the Abrahamic Covenant Chosen People within the land. When suddenly, they have left the scene by being caught up unto God, *(Revelation 12:5 & 14:1-3)* the Lord shall send forth the Two Witnesses of Enoch and Elijah for a *one-last-chance* opportunity for the Jewish people to accept His glorious invitation to become part of Christ.

"And I will give power unto my two witnesses, and they shall prophesy a thousand two hundred and threescore days; clothed in sackcloth.
These are the two olive trees, and the two candlesticks standing before the God of all the earth.

And if any man will hurt them, fire proceedeth out of their mouth, and devoureth their enemies: and if any man will hurt them, he must in this manner be killed.

These have power to shut heaven, that it rain not in the days of their prophecy: and have power over waters to turn them to blood, and to smite the earth with all plagues, as often as they will.

And when they shall have finished their testimony, the beast that ascendeth out of the bottomless pit shall make war against them, and shall overcome them, and kill them.

And their dead bodies shall lie in the street of the great city, which spiritually is called Sodom and Egypt, where also our Lord was crucified.

And they of the people and kindreds and tongues and nations shall see their dead bodies three days and a half, and shall not suffer their dead bodies to be put in graves.

And they that dwell upon the earth shall rejoice over them, and make merry, and shall send gifts one to another; because these two prophets tormented them that dwelt on the earth.

And after three days and a half the Spirit of life from God entered into them, and they stood upon their feet; and great fear fell upon them which saw them.

And they heard a great voice from heaven saying unto them, Come up hither. And they ascended up to heaven in a cloud; and their enemies beheld them."

(Revelation 11:3-12)

CHAPTER TEN

For three and one-half years, since the removing of the 144,000 *man child* constituency, the persons of Enoch and Elijah have been tormenting the Antichrist and his kingdom residents through the supernatural powers *(Revelation 11:5-6)* that they shall wield, and their righteous testimony and witness.

Christian converts, from both Jewish and Gentile backgrounds, have continued to be slaughtered within Antichrist's kingdom, and the prophesied, ever increasing Wrath of God, continues to be poured out upon a nation that declared **"his blood be upon us, and upon our children."** *(Matthew 27:25)* Yet, it seems that comparatively few individuals amongst the wicked respond, to either the righteous witness of the *Two*, or to the out-pouring of the Wrath of God. *(Revelation 9:21 & Revelation 16: 9,11)*

At the heavenly decreed moment, the righteous dead, from the whole of the *Tribulation Period* are unceremoniously raised up and whisked off to heaven to stand before the throne of God, seemingly without anyone on the Earth even consciously knowing what has happened. *(Revelation 7:15)*

And, at the end of the *Tribulation Period*, when their allotted testimony time is concluded, both Enoch and Elijah who have become spiritually *born-again* since their return to this Earth, are violently murdered. Wickedness has reached an all-time high since the days prior to the Flood of Noah. *(Genesis 6:5)*

When, after three days of unbridled revelry over their death passes, and the Holy Spirit of the Most High God enters into the deceased bodies of Enoch and Elijah, the Last Step of the *First Resurrection* and the Last Rapture shall occur.

This happens on the very same day to the very same last two individuals that make up the totality of Human Beings to be redeemed from the condition of **Spiritual Death** and become *born-again*, recreated, supernatural, New Creations of God's design. *(Revelation 20:5-6)*

They are the ones who are now destined to become the administrators and rulers, with Christ Jesus, over God's entire universe.

CHAPTER ELEVEN
The Resurrection Unto Damnation

"But the rest of the dead lived not again until the thousand years were finished." (Revelation 20:5)

The *Willy-Wonka-Golden-Ticket* invitation, to become a spiritually Born Again, Resurrected, Incorruptible, Recreated, Redeemed, Supernatural, Filled and Empowered with the Holy Spirit, Immortal, Blood-Related, Seated at the Right Hand, Household Member of the family of the Most High God, has now been withdrawn. From this time on, into all of the rest of eternity, no one else can ever be *redeemed* from the condition of **Spiritual Death**.

"Wow Pastor Rob—that's not very fair! . . . You mean that forever and ever, no one else can ever get **saved**?"

That's right.

Ladies and gentlemen, we had better come to the stark realization that we are *created creatures*. We did not orchestrate the *creation* of ourselves. We were indeed born into this world, that is true; but we did not have even the slightest input into that decision. And no matter how *smart* we may think that we are . . . we do not get to make certain eternal decisions as to what is *fair* and what is *not fair*. We can happily accept those decisions that are made by God, or we can similarly plant our feet, like an angel named Lucifer did once upon a time, and think that we should be able to sit also on the Mount of the Congregation in the sides of the north, because we know how to do it better. Although . . . that is not advisable.

We are not God. Nor will we ever be God. And the sooner that that reality breaks through to our inner-most being, the better.

The *First Resurrection* is now fully concluded. *(Revelation 20:5)* When devastating Spiritual Death entered onto the scene through Adam, and infected his progeny, God purposed to rescue His valuable *express image* Man from his sin-affected, locked-down, two-dimensional, thinking position. He invested a tremendous amount of probational *time* and energy, and took upon Himself a heinous project of pain and seeming hopelessness.

However, God faithfully saw the project through unto its triumphant completion. He has since, offered the secured results to every single person on the planet's surface, *(Romans 10:18)* whether we are aware of how He has done that, or not.

At this point in time, what more should God have to do, so that it will always be *equitable*? Possibly stop the reproduction of Mankind, so that the glorious salvation provision that He has brought forth, for the ultimate benefit of the whole of the universe, should not be *unfairly* withheld from untold future generations of Human Beings? Why don't we just allow Satan to run amok forever, throughout the universe, and continue to steal, kill, and destroy, so that the gospel can continue to be preached ad infinitum in order that people throughout the forever will still be able to get *saved*?

CHAPTER ELEVEN

Thankfully, God foreknew of the situation from *before the beginning* . . . God drafted an excellent Plan of rescue . . . God did all of the hard work concerning that Plan. The Plan itself was a tremendous success. Invitations were given to every Human Being alive ever since the successful completion of that Plan. Most invitations were sent back by the recipients, unopened. The lifeguard is soon to declare "All right, everyone out of the pool!" The pre-set probational-clock is about to sound the final alarm . . . the time has finally come, to turn out the lights.

The *Second Coming* return of Jesus Christ will produce the following five results:
1. The *Armageddon Campaign* will commence and Jesus will work his way through a number of skirmishes, ending ultimately upon the Mount of Olives. All opposing forces shall be defeated soundly as he does. *(Revelation 19:17-19)*
2. The Antichrist and his deluded side-kick, the False Prophet, shall be taken—and they shall not pass *Go* nor shall they collect *$200*—but shall be cast directly into the *Nether World* complex compartment of the Lake of Fire . . . alive. *(Revelation 19:20)*
3. Satan shall be personally bound-up with a great chain, and cast into the Bottomless Pit compartment of the *Nether World* complex, to remain incarcerated for the next 1,000 years. *(Revelation 20:1-3)*
4. Jesus shall finally be received by the Jewish Nation of Israel, and he shall be crowned as their King, to

rule over them with a rod of iron for the next 1,000 years. *(Zechariah 12:10 & Revelation 2:27 & 20:4)*

5. One of the first events after his coronation, that will be on the court calendar of King Jesus is the Judgement of the Nations. *(Matthew 25:31-46)* Rest assured that Jesus is not going to begin a 1,000 year reign of Peace-on-Earth, with vile, blaspheming, violent, Jew-hating individuals, being allowed to run free and continue to instigate their malicious terrorist activities any further.

At the very least, the leadership of any country, nation, or people that took a stand of hatred against the Hebrew people, shall stand before the King named Jesus. Be it leadership only, or populous constituency as well, they shall be judged as goats *(Matthew 25:32)*, and cast into the torment compartment called Hades, within the *Nether World* complex. *(Matthew 25:46)*

There is now finally, going to be no more war on Earth ... anywhere. There is no terrorism, no murder, no violent crimes being committed against innocent people, in various countries, throughout the globe.

The main reason for this is that Satan's kingdom of darkness on this Earth is, for all intents and purposes, paralyzed. The fallen angels and demons are all still here, but there is no active free-will operating within the kingdom of the dictator of evil; therefore, without being specifically told, no one really knows just exactly what it is that they are supposed to do. The main one who gives the orders has been temporarily jailed, and there are no orders currently being issued from

CHAPTER ELEVEN

the corporate office. With no orders being given, there is a virtual suspension of blatantly evil activities.

Various governmental necessities of men on the planet shall continue, but the current prevailing political subterfuge and lying, that goes on religiously during this 21st century, between the leaders of different countries, will abruptly come to a screaming halt at whatsoever *conference* Jesus attends.

Instructions will ultimately come forth from Jerusalem on the proper way to use the air, the water, and the soil that God has created, without poisoning them with devastating pollution.

Hidden medicinal aids and *cures* will be discovered and developed utilizing the vast amounts of flora and fauna that this planet contains.

Men and women shall continue to conduct business endeavors, remain involved in sporting activities, marry and have children, develop life-styles, and operate in all of the issues of *life* as we now know it . . . however, it will all be done under an imposed ***"rod of iron"*** regime. *(Revelation 2:27)*

One thousand years will pass just as quickly as one thousand years usually passes.

And as a foreknowledge appointed moment eventually arrives, Satan is released from the Bottomless Pit compartment of the complex, on Scriptural legalities, *(Revelation 20:3)* to once again do the only thing that he knows how to do . . . steal, kill, and destroy. *(John 10:10)*

Over the centuries that have passed, there has been a growing world-wide constituency of individuals who have become unsettled with all of the global peace and harmony that has developed under existing stringent rule, and their smoldering dissatisfactions are rising to an explosive crescendo. They are easy candidates for enlistment in the army of dissidents that the lord of darkness is building. The prevailing, two-dimensional thought process being that, if we can just enlist enough support and secure sufficient numbers, we can launch a successful assault against the instigator of this *iron-rod* oversight.

The Book reveals to us that this calculated error in judgment becomes nipped in the bud by a protective God of love, extending His hand from heaven, *(Revelation 20:9)* before the horde can even reach their intended destination.

Satan is taken and immediately plunged into the Lake of Fire, from where the Antichrist and the False Prophet have been screaming at the top of their lungs, for the last 1,000 years. *(Revelation 20:10)* And the final hour has now arrived that every single person that has ever lived on this Earth, has had an awareness of, either consciously or unconsciously . . .

Judgment Day

The Great White Throne is located in heaven, and the final trial occurs there, because these events take place in the presence of God. *(Revelation 20:12)*

The Judge who will be sitting upon the Throne is Jesus Christ of Nazareth, because all judgment has been committed unto the Son. *(John 5:22)*

The defendants in this trial are only Human Beings, who have lived from the days of Adam and Eve until now. They are all still ***Spiritually Dead***, and have the distinction of having ***Physically Died*** one time. *(Hebrews 9:27)*

The Human Beings that are alive and well on the planet Earth at the time of this Judgment, are not individuals that are personally involved with this probationary-concluding *event*. Those persons are still ***Physically Alive***, even though they are still ***Spiritually Dead***, and at some point in time during the Millennial Reign, they have been judged worthy to enter into the physical condition of 'life eternal' by the children of the Most High God. *(Matthew 25:46 & I Corinthians 6:2)*

There are no fallen angelic beings or demons at this Judgment either, because they have been judged by the *saints* at some point in time during the Millennial Reign. *(John 5:22 & I Corinthians 6:3)* *(Please remember that all **saints** are members of Christ, and are spoken of as being in **Christ** within Paul's second letter to the Corinthian church.* *(II Corinthians 6:14-16)*

Only Human Beings who have ***Physically Died*** one time are participants in this Judgment. Their spirit-soul portions of their being have been incarcerated within the *Hades* torment compartment of the *Nether World* complex *(except for the Antichrist and the False Prophet)*, but their bodies were subject to having been eaten by the fishes, burned up in the fires, rotting back to dust, or blown to smithereens. *(Revelation 20:13)*

By the knowledge and power of God, Human Triunity unity-composition shall be restored to the criminals, and each defendant shall stand before the Judge as spirit, soul, and physical body, complete. The Deed Accounting set of *books* shall be opened, and the accurate records of all thoughts, words, and deeds from the moment of their birth, shall be brought forth for each and every individual to hear. *(Revelation 20:12)*

All defendants at this spiritual trial shall have more than enough evidence, presented from the accounting *books,* to be declared *guilty*. And the judgment gavel shall fall at the conclusion of the prosecutor's presentation, and the everlasting sentence shall be decreed. However, this author chooses to believe that because we are serving a God of love and mercy that is not willing that any should perish, *(II Peter 3:9)* it shall come to pass that each individual criminal shall become acutely aware of the overwhelming amount of evidence that is being presented against them as it comes forth; and must needs come to the obvious inner conclusion. And when the moment arrives that the defendants themselves are queried concerning that evidence, each and every one shall be compelled to issue a sentence-decree of eternal condemnation upon themselves. God will effectively *send* no one to Hell, because it goes contrary to His very character of love.

The Scriptural *Second Death* that occurs for these defendants is in reality, the **Physical Death** destruction, for the second time, of their recently resurrected bodies, within the scalding cauldron of the Lake of Fire. *(Revelation 20:14)*

There is a doctrine that purports that all physical bodies shall eventually become immortal, and for those who have rebelled, those bodies shall then physically suffer for all of eternity. However, immortality and death innately do not mix . . . ever. Most of those rebels have already been suffering for centuries without their physical bodies, and the physical *Second Death* event is not going to diminish that by any means.

CHAPTER ELEVEN

Within this Lake of Fire is where the buck has finally stopped. This is where the fog-horn of finality sounds off on a regular basis, just as a reminder to all of the inhabitants of this region how truly foolish they were in their decision-making. There is no elected or appointed *overseer* within this quagmire of unending, seething hatred. Only an emanating forth of spewing blasphemy from one resident to another, as wails of burning pain and hopelessness bounce off of the cauldron walls. Teeth are heard to be gnashing from behind and within an undulating curtain of fire, as the citizens of this domain are being conformed to the *image* of their leader, with each passing minute. *(Romans 8:29)* The virus of rebellion and of misguided, exaltation promotion of the Almighty-Self is being continually sizzled and cauterized with reality and truth. And the sad reality is that there really is no bottom to this particular *pit*.

On the Earth, throughout the duration of this spiritual trial, *life* has been cruising right along. At this point in time, there are absolutely no wicked or evil people left on planet Earth . . . anywhere.

The planet has earlier been *purged* for the third time, of sins' influence. *(II Peter 3:10-12)* Natural men and women are marrying and producing children so that future colonization can begin to take place as Mankind begins to launch out into this universe that God has created for them. However, they are all still technically **Spiritually Dead**.

The visible chasm of free-will devastation consequence, that exists on the surface of this planet in the Middle East, is doing its job. *(Isaiah 66:24)* And soon the ripened fruits from the

Tree of Life will be made available to the natural-humanity constituency, to sustain regular, natural, physical body activities on into the everlasting. *(Revelation 22:2)*

The New Jerusalem, hangs suspended above the planet Earth, with the Light radiance of the Lamb of God *(Revelation 21:23)* shining through the transparent streets of gold. All spiritually Born Again, Resurrected, Incorruptible, Recreated, Filled and empowered by the Holy Spirit, Redeemed, Supernatural, Immortal, Blood-Related, Seated at the Right Hand, Household Members of the family of the Most High God reside within this city, and shall enjoy their mansions for ever more. They shall now begin to live out their creative-vision future that their Heavenly Father has planned for them since *before the beginning*, and await their executive orders for universal administration, maintenance, or governance.

Our prayer is that this little work has brought some clarity to the muddle that seems to be *out there* in these last days in which we live. Keep your eyes looking heavenward, Jesus will be here soon.

Maranatha!

SIMPLY FOR CLARITY

Raptures: (8)
1. **Enoch** (Genesis 5:24; Hebrews 11:5)
2. **Elijah** (II Kings 2:8-12; Malachi 4:5)
3. **Jesus** (Acts 1:9, 11)
4. **Many of the saints that slept** (Matthew 27:52-53)
5. **The Church of Jesus Christ** (I Thessalonians 4:16-17)
6. **The 144,000: *Man-Child* from Israel** (Revelation 12:5)
7. **The Tribulation Martyrs** (Revelation 6:9, 7:9-17, 15:2-4)
8. **The Two Witnesses: Enoch and Elijah** (Revelation 11:12)

Resurrections: (6)
1. **Jesus Christ of Nazareth** (Matthew 28:6; Mark 16:6; Luke 24:6; John 5:29, 20:19-20; Acts 13:33)
2. **Saints that slept from the Old Testament** (Matthew 27:52-53)
3. **Dead in Christ at his coming** (I Thessalonians 4:16)
4. **All the Tribulation Martyrs** (Revelation 7:9-17, 15:2-4)
5. **The Two Witnesses: Enoch and Elijah** (Revelation 11:11)
6. **All the rest of the dead, small and great** (John 5:29; Revelation 20:12-13)

MEET THE AUTHOR

By-The-Book Ministries, Inc. began in 2001 as a teaching outreach. Rob E. Daley has been gifted by God to be able to explain biblical truths in an easy to understand manner.

Many have been blessed by his teaching style.

Rob was saved and filled with the Holy Spirit in 1978 and has been instructed by the greatest teacher of all—the Spirit of Truth Himself. Rob is an ordained minister with the Assemblies of God International Fellowship and has pastored in various churches over the past 34 years.

It is the desire of this ministry to see the body of Christ solidly taught, and grow up into the things of the Lord. Rob is available for seminars, retreats, conventions, etc.

Rob can be reached at:

thedaleys@bythebookministries.org

http://robdaleyauthor.com

www.ingramcontent.com/pod-product-compliance
Lightning Source LLC
Chambersburg PA
CBHW031421040426
42444CB00005B/670